BIOLOGY

KINGFISHER

First published 2008 by Kingfisher
This revised edition published 2014 by Kingfisher
an imprint of Macmillan Children's Books
a division of Macmillan Publishers Limited
20 New Wharf Road, London N1 9RR
Basingstoke and Oxford
Associated companies throughout the world
www.panmacmillan.com

ISBN 978-0-7534-3749-0

Written by Dan Green
Consultants: Richard Walker Bsc PhD PGCE and Francesca Norris
Designed and created by Basher www.basherbooks.com
3D body illustrations (poster) by Rajeev Doshi at Medi-Mation
Cover design: Jane Tassie

Dedicated to Joyce Theobalds

Text and design copyright © Toucan Books Ltd 2008
Based on an original concept by Toucan Books Ltd
Illustration copyright © Simon Basher 2008

9 8 7 6 5 4 3 2 1
1TR/0314/WKT/SCHOY(-)/128MA

A CIP catalogue record for this book is available from the British Library.

Printed in China

Note to readers: the website address listed above is correct at the time of going to print.
However, due to the ever-changing nature of the internet, website addresses and
content can change. Websites can contain links that are unsuitable for children. The
publisher cannot be held responsible for changes in website addresses or content, or for
information obtained through a third party. We strongly advise that internet searches
should be supervised by an adult.

CONTENTS

Biology
Introduction

Biology isn't all skeletons and specimen jars – it's alive
and kicking, and crawling around in the bushes outside!
It is the study of life, taking in the animals, plants and the
stranger creatures of the world, their inner workings as
well as the minuscule cells, proteins and DNA that run
them. Life is a strange and marvellous thing. It is also still
a great mystery. There could be anything between 1.5
and 30 million species of living things on Earth. We know
a lot about the big beasts but are still in the dark about
most creepy-crawlies and microscopic bugs.

Charles Darwin was the man famous for monkeying
around with our ideas about biology. He made the most
startling of suggestions – that species (things like humans,
pigeons and daffodils) can change with time. It's a dog-
eat-dog world out there; it's also a beetle-eat-dung and
lion-eat-man world, and only the fittest survive. Those that
are best at surviving when the environment changes live
to fight another day. Darwin called this concept natural
selection, and it completely changed the way we view
the world. Sometimes the simplest ideas are the best!

Charles Darwin

Chapter 1
Building Blocks

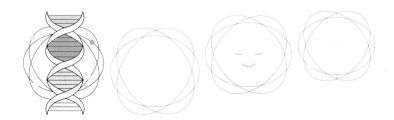

Please don't dismiss this diminutive group of tiny guys – they may be too small to see without a microscope but they hold the secrets to life itself! They run the inner workings of every living thing on Earth. The leader of the pack is the Cell, while the other Building Blocks live inside. Some of the team started out as free agents – for example, billions of years ago, Mitochondria used to live wild as a type of Bacteria – but they all now choose to work together within the Cell. The brains behind the outfit is DNA, who lives in a headquarters called the nucleus. Passing on his genes is the ultimate aim of life.

CELL

MITOCHONDRIA

DNA

RNA

RIBOSOMES

PROTEIN

Cell

Building Blocks

* The smallest living part of a protist, fungus or animal
* All life is made of these useful chaps – including your body!
* Cells are watery bags of chemicals wrapped in a protective film

You can't help but love me. I am the basic unit that all living things use to build their bodies. Every bit of you is made of me! Some living things, such as bacteria, get by with just a single cell, but you are a collection of many billions of me. My friends and I do everything for you – move, eat, think and feel. If necessary I will even die for you.

There's nothing gloomy about life in this cell. I'm a slippery bag with lots going on inside. I buzz with activity as about 100 million molecules whizz around inside me. I have a team of chemical workers, who manufacture 20,000 different substances, all vital to life. My most amazing stunt is to split myself in two and make another fully working copy of myself. This is how I construct your body from only a few hundred different types of me.

- Discoverer: Robert Hooke (1665)
- Average size: 2×10^{-5} m
- No. of cells in human body: 100 trillion

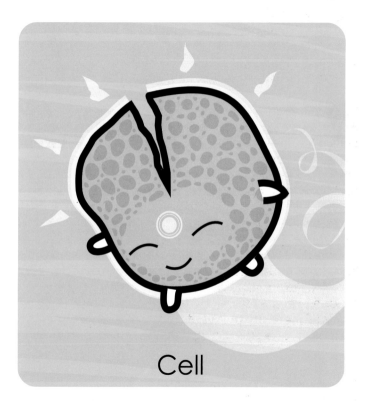

Cell

Mitochondria

Building Blocks

☀ Tiny power stations that provide the energy for most animal cells
☀ These hot rods are free workers in the cell, with their own DNA
☀ There may be hundreds of these pocket rockets inside a cell

Lean and mean, we always work at full steam! We are one of Cell's internal machines; his chief engineers. We burn food to make a superfuel called ATP. When Cell needs a boost, we smash apart the ATPs, which unleash flashes of life-giving energy. Waste not, want not; we recycle the leftover pieces back into new ATPs.

Shaped like torpedoes, we are newcomers inside cells. Two billion years ago, we may have been free-living bacteria, but we decided to join Cell's internal management and have been team members ever since. Bacteria don't use our services. We haven't given up our independence – we have our own genes, which are passed on to you via your mum. That means it's up to us when we divide and grow. When Cell needs to work harder, we boost our numbers.

● Average size: 1×10^{-6} m
● No. of genes per mitochondrion: 37
● ATPs made per second: 5 million

Mitochondria

DNA
Building Blocks

☀ Shaped as a double helix, this chemical spiral codes for life
☀ A library of info telling your body's cells how to build you
☀ This guy's full name is "Deoxyribonucleic Acid"

Some think that I'm a totally twisted individual, but while my slinky curves turn heads, I'm actually quite a bookish character. I'm so astounding that within my graceful folds and sinuous switchbacks lies the secret of life itself.

Cell has a library of me, called its genome, stored for safekeeping in the nucleus. The human library has 46 "books" in it, called chromosomes. The pages are filled with coded instructions, called genes, that are technical blueprints for making you you – from the colour of your eyes to your weakness for certain diseases. Most of the words in the books are gibberish, however, and scientists are yet to understand the purpose of this "non-coding" DNA. Although 99.9 per cent identical to all other humans, that tiny 0.1 per cent is enough to make you totally unique.

● Discoverer: Friedrich Miescher (1869)
● No. of human genes: 20,000 to 25,000
● No. of times the body's DNA is damaged per day: 10,000

DNA

RNA
Building Blocks

☀ A shadowy figure that can decode, code and copy DNA
☀ Built like DNA but without the double twist, this guy pulls the strings
☀ RNA stands for "Ribonucleic Acid"

I will always live in the shadow of my dazzling cousin, DNA. It's unfair – DNA gets all the attention for just *holding* the secrets of life. *I'm* the one who does all the work! I'm much too busy to sit around doing nothing all day like DNA. As one of the few molecules who is allowed to slip in and out of the nucleus, I can get everywhere. Like a spy selling secrets, I make a copy of DNA's genetic manual and spread it through a Cell.

I unravel DNA's double helix into two strands and then mould my body to fit with one of them. Then, with the help of Ribosomes, master code-breakers in the Cell, I follow the instructions in the manual and make the proteins that the body's workers need. Heck, some tiny viruses get away without using DNA at all!

● Date of discovery: 1939
● Average size: 3.5×10^{-7} m
● Viruses which use RNA: retroviruses, such as HIV

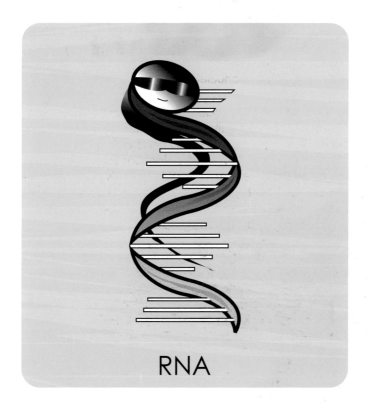

RNA

Ribosomes
Building Blocks

* A cell's protein factory that follows genetic instructions
* Controlled by strands of RNA copied from DNA
* Found in all cells, even bacteria

We're the craftsmen who build the proteins that your cells need. We may sound simple enough, but we are actually deeply complicated. We do whatever the DNA tells us; we're the only guys that can read his ancient genetic code. People often call us protein factories, but we are not large industrial plants. Instead, we are delicate workshops made of twin, interlocking parts.

A protein is a chain of smaller links called amino acids. Each gene in a piece of DNA lists the acids in the right order to make a particular protein. We assemble the sections of each protein on a production line, following the orders of RNA, who's been sent from the nucleus with a copy of a gene. Proteins are useful things. Our products might become muscles, enzymes or hormones.

● Discoverer: George Palade (1950s)
● Size: 25×10^{-9} m
● No. per cell: approximately 15,000

Ribosomes

Protein
Building Blocks

* The stuff that all life is built with – makes up and runs your body
* This super-important guy carries out all essential cell functions
* Constructed inside cells, using a kit of 20 amino acids

I am Life's "Jack-of-all-trades". I'm a no-nonsense type of geezer, well used to coping with life's problems. My skill set includes building body tissues for a dizzying range of plants and animals – muscles and membranes, fur and claws – you name it, I do it! I get things done inside cells. I read and duplicate DNA and make vast quantities of proteins to control the rate that mitochondria burn fuel. Phew!

Inside the human body I'm totally essential. I help digest your food, govern sugar levels and clot blood, to name a few of my jobs. Protein messenger-chemicals called hormones regulate the function of your organs and body processes, while enzyme proteins control chemical reactions. You get lots of me from food, but this is raw material – I've got to be built inside the body. The instructions for making me are coded into genes on DNA.

● Number of amino acids in the body: 20
● of different proteins in the human body: over 5 million
● common protein in body: collagen

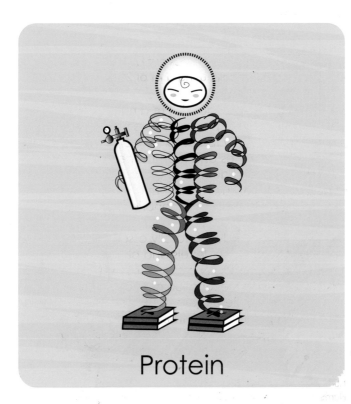

Protein

Chapter 2
Life

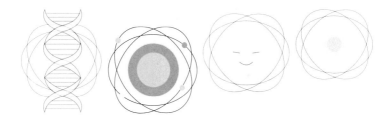

From the tiniest microscopic bacteria to gigantic, towering pine trees, this rabble is simply bursting with life! But despite the mind-boggling variety of this mob, they all do the life thing, such as getting food, using energy, building bodies and making new versions of themselves. Scientists have spent hundreds of years describing life. The biology boffins have discovered that there are five basic types of living things, so they group them into five huge collections, called kingdoms. The kingdoms are: animals, plants, fungi, bacteria and other tiny beasties called protists.

VIRUS

 BACTERIA

 PROTISTS

 FUNGUS

 SEEDLESS PLANTS

 CONIFERS

 FLOWERING PLANTS

 INVERTEBRATES

 JELLIES

 WORMS

 ARTHROPODS

 INSECTS

 MOLLUSCS

 STARFISH

 FISH

 AMPHIBIANS

 REPTILES

 BIRDS

 MAMMALS

Virus
■ Life

☀ Rogue packet of DNA or RNA that invades cells
☀ One of the smallest living things there is
☀ Responsible for many illnesses, including the common cold

I'm an itty-bitty stalker who doles out large helpings of doom. I'm a death-dealing devil and real bad news for all other living things. Sometimes I'm just a nuisance, such as when I cause a cold, chickenpox, cold sores or the rather messy winter vomiting sickness. But I can also be deadly. My dangerous forms include influenza, measles and HIV. I'm the worst kind of guest – I bust right into your body, hijack Cell and make him my slave.

I'm a tiny bandit of DNA or RNA in a protein coat. I couldn't be simpler; I barely count as a living thing. I don't eat or grow and I can't reproduce by myself. So I make Cell do it for me. I have a chemical disguise that makes me look like a friend, not foe. Luckily for you, T-Cell and the rest of the immune system are there to drive me away.

● Size: 25 to 300 x 10^{-9} m
● No. of known viruses: 5000
● Officially extinct virus: smallpox

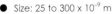

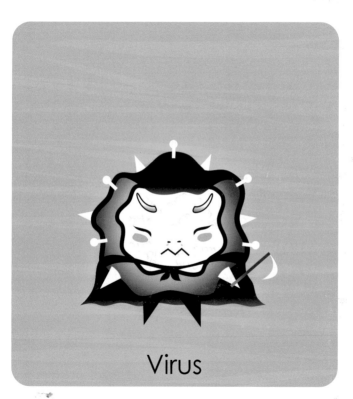

Virus

Bacteria
■ Life

* ☀ Tiny single-celled organisms that live almost everywhere
* ☀ Some of the world's worst diseases are caused by bacteria
* ☀ These minuscule guys have been around for 3.5 billion years

Our motto is "Simplicity equals success". Since the dawn of life we've done very well by not being bothered by complexity. We are tiny sacks of chemicals with none of the machinery of other types of cells, only just enough to get by. We get everywhere – literally. We hang out in rocks buried 3 km underground, chill out in nuclear waste tanks, live in boiling mud and can even survive being released into outer space! To us a dash of bleach and warm water is more dangerous than any of these.

We may be invisible, but the world couldn't live without us. We recycle all the waste and make soil fertile, and we pump out just as much oxygen as the trees. Intestines carry one kilo of us, and one trillion of us are grazing away on skin – more than there are people on Earth.

* ● Total weight of all bacteria: 150 times total weight of humans
* ● Reproductive rate: up to 28,000 copies in one day
* ● Bacterial diseases include: cholera, plague, tuberculosis

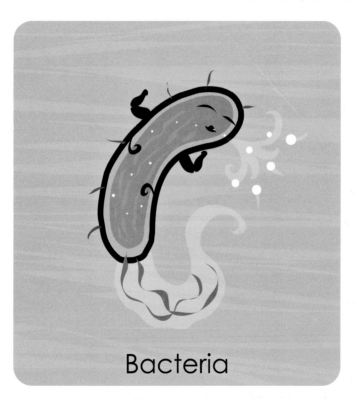

Bacteria

Protists
■ Life

✳ Living things whose bodies are made from a single cell
✳ Mostly, these guys are hundreds of times larger than bacteria
✳ Neither plants nor animals, but something in between

We are the ancient ones. Billions of years ago some of us clubbed together to become the first plants, animals and fungi. But most of us just want to be alone. We use much of the same equipment as animals and plant cells, such as mitochondria and ribosomes, but all we need to survive is a single cell – not a complicated body. But don't get us confused with bacteria!

We go by many names: amoebae, algae or protozoans. Some of us live like plants, using sunlight to make food; others are hunters that chase Bacteria through the slime, before spearing them with a barbed dart. Some of us even do both! We move in mysterious ways, too – propelled by a corkscrew tail, wafted along by hair-like cilia or simply by folding our bodies in one direction.

● Average size: 0.01 to 0.5 mm
● Deadliest protists: *Plasmodium* (malaria – causes 1 million deaths per year)
● Other diseases caused by protists: sleeping sickness, dysentery

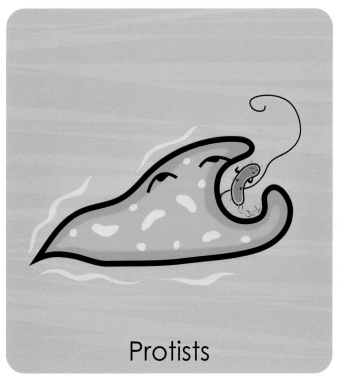

Protists

Fungus
Life

* One of a load of rotters such as mushrooms, moulds and yeasts
* Toadstools are small "fruiting bodies", which carry spores
* The real monsters lurk underground, spreading out for kilometres

I know I'm often a bit yucky but don't forget me – I have a kingdom of my own. Even so, I am the poor relation of plants and animals. You give me unlovely names like dead man's fingers, death cap and stinkhorn. Of course, that might be because I can be deadly when eaten.

You are most likely to see me in a damp forest where I send toadstools and mushrooms out into the open. But that's just the tip of the iceberg. Mostly I'm made from a mass of wispy threads that is hidden from view. And I like to spread out, sometimes covering a huge area.

I am nature's cleaner. I love dead bodies and any bits of rotting waste. I slowly devour it all, gradually turning it into sticky mush until there is nothing left.

● Food made with fungi: blue cheese, beer, bread
● Largest fungus: 9 million m^2 (honey mushroom, Oregon, USA)
● Fungal diseases include: athlete's foot, ringworm

Fungus

Seedless Plants

■ Life

☀ Ancient plants that spread to new areas using spores
☀ Include ferns, mosses and seaweeds
☀ The first types of plants to live on land

We are the ugly brothers and sisters of the plant kingdom. All of us use chlorophyll to make food from sunlight. But we don't have anything as pretty as flowers or as tasty as fruit. Some of us don't even have a leaf or root!

We are a bunch of many types of ancient plants. Some of us do like to live beside the seaside. It's not all sun and surf for seaweeds though, as they cope with being dried out and then soaked through again twice a day! Mosses and their flat mates, liverworts, were the first land plants about 475 million years ago. But 175 million years later, forests of tree ferns also covered the land. Our breeding process is quite complicated. Unlike flowering plants we breed using a sperm and an egg, not pollen. Instead of seeds we spread spores, which grow into new plants.

● Largest fronds (fern leaves): king fern (9 m long)
● Fastest-growing seaweed: giant kelp (1 m per day)
● Edible seaweeds: laverbread, Irish moss, agar jelly

Seedless Plants

Conifers
■ Life

* ☀ Evergreen trees that are the longest-living things on Earth
* ☀ Their small needle-shaped leaves can survive in icy weather
* ☀ 550 species of conifer include pines, firs and spruces

We are the biggest, toughest and longest-living plants. For many we are the symbol of Christmas, and "spruce" up the season. Where many flowering plants spend the winter looking leafless and lifeless, we keep our needle-shaped leaves all year. Even a blizzard won't get us down – our smooth diagonal sides form chutes so the heavy snow falls away. Our fast-growing trunks can be cut into planks and our wood can be pulped to make paper.

We tough it out in the extreme cold, poor soil and on high, windswept mountains. Our spiky leaves are tough and waxy so they don't dry out or freeze easily. Few animals can stomach them either. But our cones make us who we are. We invented Seed about 300 million years ago and store him inside our cones.

* ● Tallest conifer: coast redwood (115.2 m)
* ● Thickest trunk: Montezuma cypress (11.42 m diameter)
* ● Oldest conifer: Great Basin bristlecone pine (4700 years old)

Conifers

Flowering Plants
■ Life

* ☀ Show-offs who bring flowers, pollen and fruit into the world
* ☀ Many scented and colourful plants are lifelong pals with insects
* ☀ For 130 million years they have been the main plants on Earth

Before we came on the scene, the world must have been a dull place. Conifers are so stern and stiff (and they all look so similar), and the Seedless Plants are all dressed in drab greens and browns. We are fabulous though – real stunners – and bring colour to the Earth.

We are very image-conscious. Our flowers' arrangements of colour and perfume attract animals. We want them to pay us a visit so we can get them to carry pollen to our neighbours. But some of us, such as grass, are content to bend with the wind – that will spread pollen just as well. We are also important to you humans. A lot of your food comes from us – wheat and rice, corn and oats, most vegetables, peas and beans, oils, fruits and nuts. We even provide the cotton fibres for your clothes.

* ● Scientific name: angiosperms
* ● Earliest known flower: *Archaefructus liaoningensis* (125 million years ago)
* ● Largest flowering plant: *Eucalyptus amygdalina* (125 m)

Flowering Plants

Invertebrates

■ Life

☀ The first animals to evolve at least 650 million years ago
☀ Animals with no backbone who colonized land first
☀ Include the world's tiniest beasts but some monsters, too

Although you think of us as spineless simpletons, we rule the world. Get over yourselves, you big-boned blunderers, we make up 97 per cent of all animal species on Earth!

We include everything from tiny plankton floating in the sea to giant squids, the original sea monsters that are longer than most boats. In between are all sorts of soft jellies and slimy worms. Some of us, such as clams and Starfish, are hard cases who are banged up in shells – for life! Our largest group is the armour-plated Arthropods.

For our size we beat most vertebrates hands down – even though we don't have any hands, of course. We have world-beating jumpers and weightlifters, and we hold the world land-speed record, too. Beat that!

● Highest jumper: froghopper (jumps 70 times its height)
● Best weightlifter: rhinoceros beetle (lifts 850 times its weight)
● Fastest runner: American cockroach (runs 50 times its own length per second)

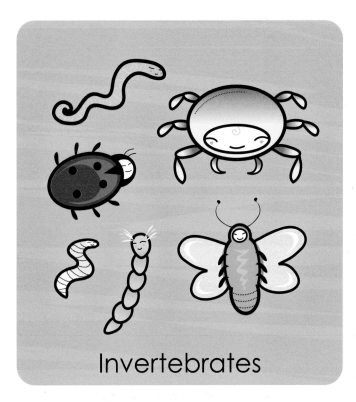

Invertebrates

Jellies
■ Life

* Brainless wonders with circular bodies and trailing tentacles
* Food and waste come in and out through the same hole
* Include jellyfish, sea anemones and corals

We're 98 per cent water, but we're not drips! We might be almost invisible, but some of us have a sting in our tails. Your best chance of seeing us is when we crowd together in a bloom. In the dark, deep sea we put on a light show, too. Home-making corals huddle together in their billions forming massive reefs. Australia's Great Barrier Reef is even visible from Space.

Jellies

● Deadliest jelly: box jellyfish
● Largest jelly: lion's mane (2 m wide)
● No. of species: 9000

Worms

Life

* Include leeches, terrifying tapeworms and grimy earthworms
* Divided into segmented worms, roundworms and flatworms
* At least 55,000 species and they're all completely legless

Worms

Let's face it, we can't afford to be fussy. We're happy to live almost anywhere. With no backbone for support, we grow largest in water, but we also wriggle through soil, of course. If you are very unlucky we might be wriggling inside your blood or intestines, too. We are found in other inhospitable places, even hot water belched from seabed volcanoes!

- Longest worm: ribbon worm (50 m)
- No. of earthworms: up to 500 per square metre of soil
- No. of segments in an earthworm: 150

Arthropods

■ Life

☀ Creepy-crawlies with a skeleton on the outside, not the inside
☀ Include insects, spiders, scorpions and crabby crustaceans
☀ Evolved in the sea before becoming the first land animals

Welcome to the Age of the Arthropod! Over 84 per cent of all animals on this planet belong in our mind-boggling collection of Invertebrates. We evolved from worms somewhere out there on the seabed more than half a billion years ago. Our name means "jointed legs", and we've got lots of them. Most of us are Insects with a measly six limbs, but scuttling millipedes have 200-plus!

We all have bodies formed in sections. Unlike vertebrates, which hang their squidgy parts on an internal skeleton, we keep our soft bits safe in a suit of armour called an exoskeleton. Our feelers do a lot more than feel – some of us smell with them, too. We see the world differently from you. Spiders, for example, have eyes in the back of their heads!

● Edible arthropods include: prawns, lobsters, crabs
● Largest arthropod: spider crab (6.4 kg, 3.8 m across)
● Smallest arthropod: *Eriophyid* mite (0.15 mm)

Arthropods

Insects

■ Life

* Six-legged arthropods that get almost everywhere
* Three-quarters of all known animal species are insects
* More than 1 million types have been found, and still counting

We are the biggest gang of Arthropods. Insects rule! We are masters of air and land. The salty ocean waves are the only place we don't thrive, but we're working on it!

There is a lot more to us than buzzy wasps that spoil a picnic or vibrant butterflies that flit around the garden. Many of us are hidden from view: beetles are toiling in the soil, busy ants are labouring underground and cockroaches are getting mucky in rubbish tips.

One of the secrets of our success is that our kids don't get in the way. Most insect young spend their days as worm-like grubs, maggots and caterpillars. These larvae do nothing but eat and grow. Then it's time to transform into glorious adults and the race is on to find a mate.

● Heaviest insect: giant weta (70 g)
● Estimated no. of undiscovered species: 30 million
● Deadliest insects: mosquitoes carrying malaria

Insects

Molluscs

■ Life

* Around 128,000 species who mainly live in the sea
* Slugs and snails are the only land-going molluscs
* Many molluscs carry their protective shell-houses with them

We do our best to look like tough, hard cases, but inside we're real softies. It is not always obvious we are related – we've got snails, oysters, cockles and mussels in our clan. Some of us sift food from water with a snotty net; the rest of us scrape up food with a jagged cutting tool called a radula. The largest (and brainiest) molluscs of all are octopuses and squids.

Molluscs

● Largest mollusc: colossal squid (14 m)
● Deadliest mollusc: blue-ringed octopus
● Largest shellfish: giant clam (137 cm)

- ✵ A prickly bunch with skeletons made of calcium, a bit like bone
- ✵ Adults move using a system of water pumps that power tubular feet
- ✵ Babies swim freely in the water; adults are normally seabed bound

Starfish

Excuse us, darling, VIPs coming through! We're the stars of the sea. Our many arms drip with jewel-like spines, we bring colour to the drab rock and sand of the seabed. We are pretty special. We can change colour and will grow a new arm if an annoying snapper breaks one off. Other members of the family include unruly spiked sea urchins and bland sea cucumbers.

- ● Largest number of arms: *Helicoilaster* (50)
- ● Heaviest starfish: *Thromidia catalai* (6 kg)
- ● Poisonous starfish: crown-of-thorns

Fish

■ Life

* ☀ The largest group of vertebrates with about 25,000 species
* ☀ A wet lot that breathe underwater using gills
* ☀ Many food fish are in danger from greedy overfishing

When we arrived on the scene 500 million years ago, we caused a splash! We were the first animals with backbones and we've been braving the waters ever since.

We range from the deep ocean to rivers and flooded caves. We are the world's top swim team – most of us have a gas bag called the swim bladder to keep us afloat. We don't have legs, just fins, but a few of us can flip-flop about on land, and some can even fly!

Most of us have skeletons made from tiny, sharp bones. Watch out, they might get stuck in your throat. But one notorious gang of fierce fish – led by the sharks – are completely boneless. They use rubbery cartilage instead. Watch out you don't get stuck in *their* throats!

* ● Fastest fish: sailfish (100 km/h)
* ● Longest-living fish: beluga sturgeon (over 100 years)
* ● Largest fish: whale shark (25 tonnes)

Fish

Amphibians

■ Life

* Bulging-eyed slimeballs that live near water
* Of the 6000 species, most are frogs and toads
* Thin-skinned and cold-blooded, many are endangered species

We are a group of secretive, sun-shy creatures. Take some time to get to know us and you'll love us, warts and all! As well as leaping frogs and waddling toads, we include salamanders, newts and blind, legless chaps called caecilians. We live in damp places because we breathe through our skin and need to keep it moist and fresh.

We were the first vertebrates to try life on land, 400 million years ago. Since then, we've been commuting between land and water. Some of us never leave the water even now, and our fishy past is there for all to see in the jelly-covered eggs we lay, always in or close to water. Our babies are born with gills and spend their childhood in water. Once we've grown lungs we can hunt on land. Watch out Insects. Here we come!

* Largest frog: goliath frog (30 cm; weighs as much as a pet cat)
* Largest leap: tree frogs can jump 20 times their own length
* Most poisonous frog: golden poison dart frog

Amphibians

Reptiles
■ Life

* 7700 species include turtles, crocodiles, lizards and snakes
* A bunch of sun-worshippers with dry, scaly skin
* Most young hatch from eggs with soft but waterproof shells

We're most likely to be found lying out in the sunshine. There's nothing we love better than soaking up some rays. We're not at our best in the morning – our cold blood means that we're sluggish starters, and we have to wait to warm up before we can get down to a day's business. But we can afford to lie in – we only need to eat about a fifth as much as the hot-bodied mammals and birds to keep our bodies in working order.

We might look lazy but don't be fooled: we have a long history. Way back, our dinosaur cousins ruled the world. Perhaps our glory days are gone – but some of us are still at the top of our game: you'll know what we mean if you ever get eye-to-eye with a grinning crocodile or meet a death-dealing cobra with syringe-like fangs.

● Largest reptile: saltwater crocodile (over 6 m)
● Smallest reptile: dwarf sphaero gecko (16 mm)
● Longest-living reptile: giant tortoise (over 170 years)

Reptiles

51

Birds
Life

- 10,000 species of flappers and flyers that evolved from dinosaurs
- Feathered friends that lay tough-shelled eggs
- These colourful twitterers fill the world with song

The sky's the limit for us fly guys! We soar effortlessly through the air while you plodders stay rooted to the ground! Though known for flying, some of us are swift runners and others are ace swimmers. We're all built to the same template – two legs, two wings, waterproof feathers and warm blood. We need to keep our weight down, and have hollow bones filled with air and a horny beak instead of heavy teeth. Our beaks are shaped according to our food but without gnashers we need help to chop up our meals. That is why you find us pecking around for grit – it grinds up the food in our churning tums.

We like crowds and sometimes flock together in our hundreds of thousands. Many of us take a winter holiday every year, flying off to sunnier lands to escape the cold.

- Fastest flier: eider duck (270 km/h)
- Smallest bird: bee hummingbird (5 cm)
- Highest flier: Ruppell's gryphon vulture (11,000 m)

Birds

Mammals

■ Life

* ✸ Fur-covered animals that feed their babies with milk
* ✸ Nearly half of the 4600 species are rats and other rodents
* ✸ The world's most famous mammal is reading this book now

We're the top dogs of the animal kingdom – and the top cats, skunks and llamas, too. Over the last 60 million years or so, we've made this little planet our own – we can survive more or less everywhere apart from the icy wastes of Antarctica and the deepest ocean floors.

You couldn't get a more diverse lot of beasts than us. We are both the hunters and the hunted, often fighting with tooth and claw. We are bears and bats, dolphins and deep-diving whales, tiny mice and enormous elephants, kangaroos, cows and the kooky duck-billed platypus. But we have more in common than our hair. Our kids are born live (apart from two or three weirdo egg-laying types called monotremes) and our first meals are always drinks of warm milk straight from our mum.

* ● Fastest mammal: cheetah (95 km/h over 500 m)
* ● Largest mammal: blue whale (190 tonnes)
* ● Venomous mammals: duck-billed platypus, solenodon, water shrew

Mammals

Chapter 3
Body Bits

This crew of hard-working, heavy-duty fellas operate a fantastically complicated machine – you! They are an all-star outfit who gel together perfectly to make running your body processes a breeze. Every member of this team is an expert with a certain area of responsibility. Some are part of a system that controls one function of the body, such as moving, eating or getting rid of waste. Others are organs – fleshy factories that make or collect the things the body needs to survive. And they are all made from trillions of individual cells. There are nearly 7 billion people on Earth and all of them are made the same way – just like you!

 HEART

 RED BLOOD CELL

 B-CELL

 T-CELL

 LUNGS

 SKELETON

MUSCLE

 BRAIN

 NERVOUS SYSTEM

 TONGUE

 NOSE

EYE

EAR

 TOUCH

 HORMONES

 SPERM

 EGG

 BABY IN WOMB

 STEM CELL

 TOOTH

 STOMACH

 INTESTINES

 LIVER

 KIDNEY

 BLADDER

 SKIN

 NAILS

 HAIR

Heart

Body Bits

- ✹ A fist-sized organ that pumps blood around your body
- ✹ This tireless muscle man sits just to the left in your chest
- ✹ When this guy gets ill, the rest of the body can't keep going

I'm a pounding Muscle beating at the very core of your existence. I am officially your body's hardest-working part. I pump 8000 litres of blood every day. And I never stop or get tired.

If I do stop beating, you're in trouble. Brain can only survive for a few minutes without the life-giving oxygen that I pump around the body. My double-pump system sends blood to the Lungs first, to power up on oxygen, then it returns to me and I send it shooting around the body to Cell and his friends. The pressure I generate in your arteries is enough to squirt blood across the room. But I'm a sensitive guy – when you get scared or nervous I beat faster. I also make you blush, by pumping blood into Skin.

- ● Adult heart rate: 75 beats per minute
- ● Blood pumped in 1 year: 3 million litres
- ● No. of heartbeats in a lifetime: 1 to 3 billion

Heart

Red Blood Cell

Body Bits

* Live-fast-die-young hero who gives blood its red colour
* A round cell with no nucleus, who is full of iron
* Busy chap who carries oxygen around the body

I'm a breath of fresh air for your body. I'm a specialist, trained for one thing only – to bring life-giving oxygen to Cell whenever and wherever he needs it.

I use an iron-rich chemical called haemoglobin to pick up the oxygen from Lungs. When I'm full of oxygen, I am bright scarlet. When the blood is full of carbon dioxide waste thrown out by Cell, I appear much darker.

Just one drop of blood has about 5 million of me in it, so imagine how many there are in the 5 litres that pump around your body. I'm made in the marrow inside bones, which pumps out 2 million new versions of me every second. When I'm old, Liver will break me down and my red colour will end up as the yellow in urine.

● Discoverer: Jan Swammerdam (1658)
● Average size: 7×10^{-6} m
● Average lifespan: 4 months

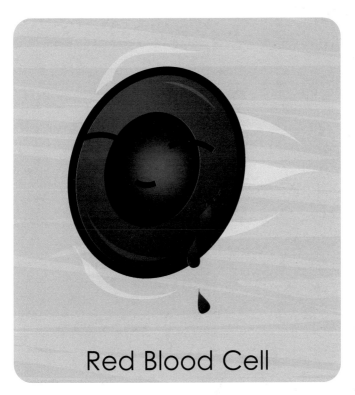

Red Blood Cell

B-Cell
Body Bits

☀ A white blood cell that protects you from future invasion
☀ Patrols the blood and lymphatic system looking for trouble
☀ Highlights dangerous invaders with markers called antibodies

I am your body's police officer. I look out for trouble and raise the alarm when dangerous invaders appear. I can remember what they all look like from the last time they made you ill. But I make sure you won't get fooled again. I release chemical flags that plant themselves on the invaders. Tough T-Cell knows just what my markers mean: "Kill this now!"

B-Cell

● B stands for: Bursa of Fabricius
● Other name: B-lymphocyte
● Cancer of the B-Cells is lymphoma

T-Cell
Body Bits

* A white blood cell working in the immune system
* A member of your body's special forces, trained to kill invaders
* Does battle in the lymphatic system and blood

T-Cell

I'm a natural-born killer. I cruise around your body's blood vessels looking for nasty invaders, such as viruses. When you get ill there can be as many as 7000 of me in one drop of blood. My weapons are designed to kill a certain invader, such as a flu virus. B-Cell guides me to the right target. When the trouble is over, I am deactivated to stop me causing havoc.

- T stands for: thymus
- Other name: T-lymphocyte
- Disease of the T-Cells: HIV (AIDS) attacks them

Lungs
Body Bits

* A pair of gas bags sitting on either side of your chest
* Spongy lobes that suck in oxygen and breathe out waste gas
* The total surface area inside is as large as a tennis court

We are a set of beautiful twins that give your body a good airing. Life's a gas for us – we take oxygen from the air and pass it to Red Blood Cell. At the same time we get rid of suffocating carbon dioxide waste.

We suck air in with the help of a muscular pump called the diaphragm, which rises and falls on top of your liver and intestines. On the way in, your nose and throat clean and moisten the air. Once inside, the air rushes into sacs called alveoli. There are 300 million of them inside us, each one covered in tiny blood vessels. This is where we do the switch: oxygen in and carbon dioxide out. We're made of pink foamy flesh, but if you smoke, you'll make us a sooty mess, turning a softly purring machine into wheezing windbags.

* Average capacity: 5 litres
* Length of lung's airways: 2400 km
* Resting breathing rate: 15 times per minute

Lungs

Skeleton

Body Bits

* A super group of 206 bones
* These upright guys provide a framework for your body
* The longest bones are in your leg; the smallest are in the ear

I am the body's super-tough hard case and it's my job to protect and support. I am the superstructure where the rest of the body bits hang out – without me you'd be nothing more than a floppy pile of flesh.

My bones are stronger than steel and can carry five times my own weight. I achieve this with a magic mix of flexible collagen fibres and the rock-hard mineral calcium phosphate. Ties called ligaments join my bones together. I can crack from time to time, but I can mend myself with my powers of regeneration.

Like Italian cannelloni pasta, my bones are hollow and filled with mush. It's called marrow. This stuff makes 175 billion new red blood cells per day.

● Total weight of skeleton: about 9 kg
● Most bones broken in a lifetime: 433 (Evel Knievel)
● No. of bones in spine: 26

Skeleton

Muscle
■ Body Bits

☀ The muscle man who keeps your body on the move
☀ A bundle of protein filaments that shortens when electrified
☀ Meat is the muscles of animals, such as cows and chickens

Skeleton always tries to take the credit for keeping you upright, but without me all it can do is stand still. That bag of old bones just provides anchor points for me and the 649 other muscles to do the real work.

Once I've got my instructions from Nervous System I work by contracting tiny bundles of fibres, so they get shorter and fatter. I can only pull, not push, so I often work in pairs to tug Skeleton's lazy bones around. For example, your biceps bend your arm at the elbow, and your triceps, on the other side of the bone, straighten it.

Skeletal muscles do the moving and lifting work. Smooth muscles are automatic and power Bladder and Intestines. Heart's muscles never get tired!

● Largest muscle: gluteus maximus (buttocks)
● No. of muscles required to smile: 12
● No. of muscles required to frown: 11

Muscle

Brain
Body Bits

- This clever character controls all your body processes
- A softy made of electrified grey matter and white matter
- The location of the mind, where you do your thinking

It's a no-brainer: I am the most important organ. All the body crew claim that they are indispensable, but I'm the only one you can't replace. I control you. Remove your hard hat – the skull – and underneath you will find a juicy, wrinkly blob. Your hind- and midbrain, at the back, control automatic stuff like breathing and balance.

The forebrain is a whirl of activity that lets you be a fully functioning individual. This part of me lets you talk, have hare-brained ideas and laugh at jokes. The information from your five senses is processed here. On good days, I'm also capable of some independent thought, too! All this brain work takes a lot of resources. I use up a fifth of the oxygen taken in by the lungs and I have my own dedicated blood supply.

- Average weight: 1.4 kg
- No. of nerve cells: 100 billion
- No. of connections with each cell: between 10 and 10,000

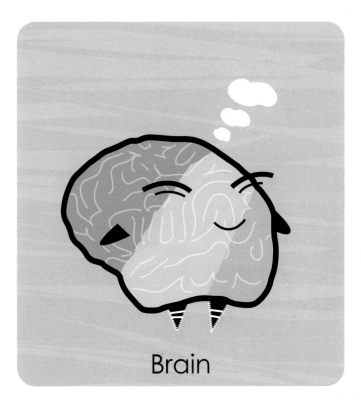

Brain

Nervous System
Body Bits

* A sensitive guy who feels your pain
* This guy is a live wire and does things without thinking
* A whole-body network that reacts like greased lightning

I'm a sparky chap. I am your communication network filled with signals of electric pulses. I connect your early warning system to Brain and then carry his commands to Muscle – in case you need to make a quick getaway.

My billions of branches cover the entire surface of your body with sensitive nerve endings that detect Touch, pain and heat. I also carry messages from your team of detectors – Eyes, Ears, Nose and Tongue – to your Brain.

Most of my branches lead back to the spinal cord, which is the body's central information cable. Brain does all the thinking, but reflex actions, like flinching away from a hot surface, are controlled by the cord alone.

● Total length of nerves: 150,000 km
● Speed of nerve signal: 120 metres per second
● Voltage of nerve signal: 30 mV

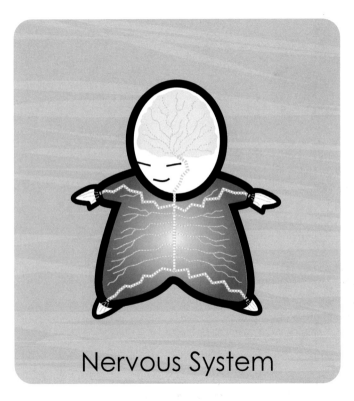

Nervous System

Tongue
Body Bits

☀ Sensitive buds on the tongue pick up chemicals in your food
☀ Used to decide whether food is dangerous or full of goodness
☀ Powerful tongue muscles can't be licked for strength

I am the centre of operations for your sense of taste. And I'm not a pretty sight – to an outsider I am a slobbery, drooling wriggler covered in stinky Bacteria, but I think I'm made in the best possible taste.

I'm not just used for sloshing food around between the teeth, although my furry surface helps me grip even the gooiest of snacks. (I'm also a star player in the speech team – without me they'd be in trouble.) But my pride and joy are the thousands of little lumps that run from my tip, down my sides and around my back. These buds handle simple tastes like sweet, sour, salty and bitter, as well as a lesser known fifth taste, called umami, or "meatiness". But I'm no expert compared to Nose. Normally, he checks out food first.

● Longest human tongue: 9.5 cm from lips to tip when stuck out of the mouth
● Lifespan of taste buds: 10 days
● Scientific name for taste: gustation

Tongue

75

Nose
Body Bits

* This sensitive fellow runs a chemical detection system
* Has a hair-like lining that sniffs out smells
* Scientists refer to the sense of smell as olfaction

I sometimes look down at things, but that is the only way I know how to work. You'd do well to follow me. I use chemical sensors deep inside me to pluck scents from the air. People rely on sight so much, I get overlooked, but smell is one of your strongest senses. I'm 10,000 times more sensitive than brutish Tongue. I get you licking your lips before you even realize you're hungry.

My odour detectives are hair-shaped cilia that line chambers inside me. Each cilium looks out for certain chemicals swirling around in the air you breathe and sends a signal to Brain. The cilia are sensitive souls – think of that next time you go rooting around inside me with a finger! Cilia like being damp, but a snotty cold swamps them with mucus, so they barely work at all.

● Sensitivity of nose: it can detect 10,000 different smells
● Wind speed of a sneeze: 63 km/h
● Size of the cilia zone: 2.5 cm^2

Nose

Eye
■ Body Bits

- ☀ A squishy light-sensor that brings things into focus
- ☀ Its inner lining is sensitive to different light frequencies
- ☀ Sight is controlled by the visual cortex at the back of the brain

I'm a true visionary – a squishy ball of clear gel that is your window on the world. I'm used for sight, the principal sense for most people. Gaze deeply into me and you will discover just how complex I really am.

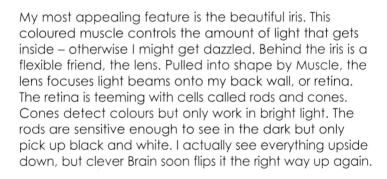

My most appealing feature is the beautiful iris. This coloured muscle controls the amount of light that gets inside – otherwise I might get dazzled. Behind the iris is a flexible friend, the lens. Pulled into shape by Muscle, the lens focuses light beams onto my back wall, or retina. The retina is teeming with cells called rods and cones. Cones detect colours but only work in bright light. The rods are sensitive enough to see in the dark but only pick up black and white. I actually see everything upside down, but clever Brain soon flips it the right way up again.

- ● No. of rods: 120 million
- ● No. of cones: 7 million
- ● Eyelids: wipe eyes clean and keep them moist

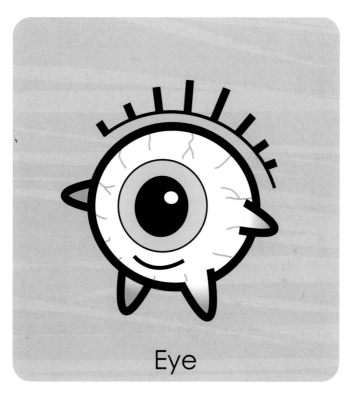

Eye

Ear
■ Body Bits

- ☀ A funnel-shaped dishy guy that collects sound waves
- ☀ Sound waves are converted into electric pulses inside
- ☀ Also used to help you stay balanced

I am your body's hi-fi system – a finely tuned sensor that picks up the tiniest vibration in the air. Thanks to me you can experience these vibrations as sweet sounds.

My outer section channels air waves into your earhole – and then the real business begins. The air beats on a drum of Skin, and the rhythm is passed through a skiffle group of tiny bones to a shell of bone called the cochlea. The cochlea is full of fluid. Every beat sends a ripple through the fluid, which is picked up by microscopic hairs. The hairs are connected to Nervous System, who carries a signal to Brain. He'll let you know if I hear anything interesting. I'm also well-balanced – the inner ear has chambers of jelly that detect changes in body position and give you a sense of what's up and down.

- ● Length of smallest ear bone (stirrup): 3 mm
- ● Speed of sound waves: 332 metres per second
- ● Adult ear's sensitivity: 20 to 20,000 Hertz

Ear

Touch

Body Bits

- A touchy-feely sense who can also be a right pain!
- Uses nerve endings in skin to sense pressure and temperature
- The most touch-sensitive places are fingertips and lips

Give me a hug, I'm the forgotten sense. I'm at work on every inch of your body and often get overlooked. But I have so many skills – I can feel hot and cold and a whole range of pushes, pinches and pinpricks. However, I sometimes get my own back – when I'm feeling itchy and scratchy you can't think about anything but me!

I'm right under your skin, where the nerves are plugged into sensors. Tiny hairs in Skin detect the slightest brush or breeze. Another detector looks out for heat, while a separate type feels the cold. Deeper down, nerve endings detect pressure. If my system gets overloaded, I'll send out pulses of pain to warn you of danger. My fabulous system also tells Brain how your body is positioned, so you don't have to think about it.

- Speed of pain signal: 30 metres per second
- Visceral sensors: pick up stomach aches and other internal pains
- Scientific name: somatosensory system

Touch

83

Hormones
Body Bits

* Moody fellows who regulate your body functions
* Chemical messengers that work with the nervous system
* Produced by glands in several areas of the body

I get my name from the Greek word "horman", meaning "to set in motion" – I make things happen. Your body functions may be all Greek to you, but without me nothing would get done. I am produced by squishy lumps called glands, which squirt different types of me into your bloodstream. Like a courier, I speed towards my target destination with a list of instructions. Once there, I encourage Cell to start doing things differently.

There isn't much I don't do, actually. I control the way you use energy and water. I have a role in how you sleep, and I affect your moods. One important job is reorganizing your body as it matures into an adult. That's not easy. Sometimes I overreact a little and cause a problem or two. But you get used to it; it's all part of growing up.

● No. of hormones in the body: over 50
● Well-known hormones: insulin, adrenaline, testosterone, oestrogen
● Largest hormone gland: thyroid

Hormones

85

Sperm

Body Bits

* A little squirt who wants to meet Egg
* Carries an X or Y chromosome to decide the sex of a baby
* His name is short for "spermatozoon"

I'm a little guy with a big job. Along with my other half, Egg, I make new life. There are no other cells like us – we can't copy ourselves and we carry only half a set of DNA each. When we meet, we fuse our half-sets to make a unique genetic combo – a new human being.

I won't get anywhere unless I am fast – it's a race to reach Egg before she gets too old. And I have to be the first. I'm a champion swimmer with a long tail. My life is brief but glorious. I start out in one of the two testes, a man's Sperm factories, and travel upstream towards the penis. As I pass the prostate gland, fluids get added, which gives me fuel for my journey. If everything is going swimmingly, I enter a female body and it takes an hour or so to get to Egg.

● Swimming speed: 1 to 3 mm/minute
● No. produced per day: 50 to 500 million
● Length: 50×10^{-6} m

Sperm

Egg
Body Bits

* ☀ Sperm's life partner; together they bring babies into the world
* ☀ The female sex cell; its proper name is ovum
* ☀ The largest cell made by the human body

I'm infinitely precious and pregnant with possibility. I'm born in a woman's ovary and once a month I float like a miniature balloon towards her womb to make a date with Sperm – if he turns up! Men make millions of Sperm every day, but I'm much rarer. A woman will release just 400 of me in a lifetime.

I'm one big mama – 85,000 times bigger than Sperm – but there is a lot more to me. I have a half-set of DNA like my male counterpart, but I also have a full team of workers, such as Mitochondria and Ribosomes – everything that is needed to power my growth into a baby if I fuse with Sperm. The uterus gets ready to nurture the new life, but if Sperm doesn't arrive, I leave during a period.

* ● Average size: 1.5×10^{-4} m
* ● Lifespan after release: 24 hours
* ● Egg + Sperm = zygote

Egg

Baby in Womb
Body Bits

- This little tyke is a model of good breeding
- Grown from a single cell inside the womb, or uterus
- Supplied by a fuel pipe called the umbilical cord

I don't know much really – I haven't even been born yet – even so, I think I might be the most amazing thing that the human body can do. When Sperm and Egg get together on the way to a woman's womb, it's just the beginning of an incredible journey, one that results in a whole new person being created.

The single cell, or zygote, formed from Sperm and Egg splits in two over and over again to make a ball of cells, which glues itself to the womb. In a month I have a million cells and have formed them into two teams: one side becomes an embryo with buds for arms, legs and everything else. The rest is the placenta, a fuelling depot that supplies me with food. After nine months, I've had enough – it's time to meet the world.

- New babies per year: 130 million
- Uterus size: expands to 500 times its original size
- Chances of twins: one in 70 births

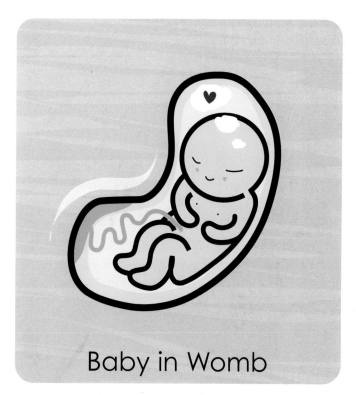

Baby in Womb

Stem Cell

Body Bits

* A mighty morphing power cell that can grow into anything
* Found in embryos, bone marrow, the liver and the eye
* Could one day be used to build replacement body parts

I am the special one. I'm not like any other cell – Brain's cells are always brain cells, and Red Blood Cell can never become anything else, but I can be anything I want to be. I can grow into any type of cell I choose... or just keep reproducing without making a firm decision. One day I'll choose my path and grow into a liver cell, skin cell or something else. I have so much potential!

My talents make me incredibly valuable. Because I can become anything from kidney to muscle to heart cells, I could one day be used to build replacement organs. Transplants or grafts grown from me in the lab will be easy to fit. I could even be used to mend faulty DNA, which causes some of the world's most terrifying diseases, such as Alzheimer's or Parkinson's.

● Discoverers: Ernest McCulloch and James Till (1960s)
● Most common in: growing babies in the womb
● Adult stem cells: located in bone marrow and skin

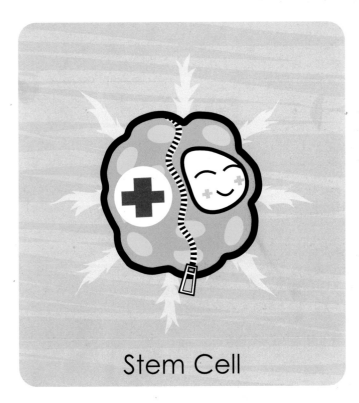

Stem Cell

93

Tooth

Body Bits

- A tough guy who shreds the morsels you eat
- This choppy fella is a human's hardest part
- Needs brushing twice a day to scrub away nasty bacteria

Along with the body's strongest muscle – in the jaw –
and a mouthful of friends, there's not much that I can't
demolish. I am built in three layers. First is a tough, white
outer casing called enamel. Then comes a filler called
dentine, and finally pulp. Your mouth is home to lots of
bacteria. Their waste products eat away at my enamel.
I should feel no pain because all my nerves are buried
deep down, but if bacteria break in, I'll ache for sure.

I come in four different shapes. Nippers called incisors live
at the front of the mouth. Then come canines – fangs for
stabbing food. The wide-boys on each side are premolars
and molars – they bump and grind the food into a paste.
The largest molars sit at the back. You don't get these
four huge "wisdom" teeth until you are a real grown-up.

- No. of baby teeth: 20
- No. of adult teeth: 32
- No. of bacteria in mouth: over 6 million

94

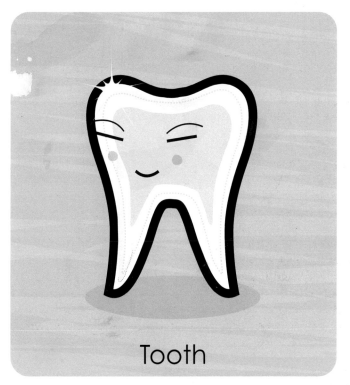

Tooth

Stomach
Body Bits

* A rotund fellow who loves a filling meal
* A well-muscled bag filled with acid and a few bacteria
* An acid-bath where food breaks down

I've got a bad rep – I'm always to blame for people being too heavy. But I put up with some pretty unpleasant working conditions just to bring you the juicy goodness from the food you scoff. The stomach juices that sluice around inside me are acidic enough to burn your skin, and I am home to an enzyme called pepsin, which breaks down proteins.

My job is to mash up your food and turn it into a thick gloop called chyme. My interior is lined with a mucus layer that stops the vicious acid burning. If that stops working a painful ulcer will form. I can "stomach" pretty much anything, but when something doesn't agree with me, a series of quick muscular contractions send it back out the way it came in!

● Time food is in stomach: about 90 minutes to 4.5 hours
● Stomach acid: 10 times stronger than vinegar
● Capacity of stomach: 1.5 litres

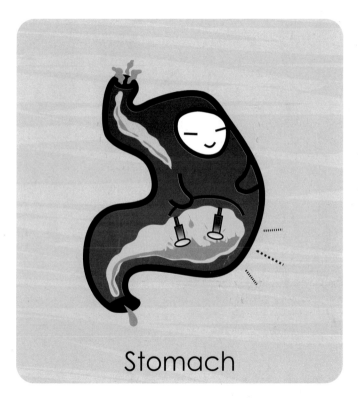

Stomach

Intestines
Body Bits

* A long tube snaking through your middle
* Food moves through this pipe with muscular jerks and spasms
* Nutrients from the food pass through the wall into the blood

I'm a gutsy performer, the business end of your body's fabulous food-processing facility. Like a squirming serpent I lie coiled in your belly. As churned-up nosh makes its way around my long and winding loops, I use a variety of cunning tricks to suck all the best stuff from it. What's left once I've finished is pongy waste. It's the dirtiest job in the body, but someone's got to do it.

Although I'm on the inside, I'm actually an outer layer of the body – like the hole running through a very long doughnut. I'm in two sections. The small intestine is a narrow pipe where food is processed. The waste moves into the large intestine. The water is sucked out, leaving a whiffy mixture of solid and gas, which leaves the body through the anus.

● Length of small intestine: 6 m
● Length of large intestine: 1.5 m
● Time food spends in intestines: 12 hours

Intestines

Liver
Body Bits

* A wobbly workaholic who cleans up after the rest of the body
* This hothouse of activity generates heat for your body
* Just pips the brain to the post as the body's heaviest organ

I'm a multi-tasker, a jack-of-all-trades and master of every single one. If you want something done, I'm your man. With over 500 jobs on my list, I always "de-liver"! There's so much going on inside my four floppy lobes that scientists don't know the half of what I do.

I collect nutrients from blood and store essential vitamins and iron. On top of that I act like a cleaner, removing poisons as well as damaged red blood cells from your blood. I send all this waste down the line to Kidney for throwing away. I'm also responsible for breaking down fat and cholesterol. Could you live without me? Well, obviously not, but you could live without 90 per cent of me. I have amazing regenerative powers and can grow back from just a tiny blob.

● Average weight: 1.4 to 1.6 kg
● Proportion of body weight: 2 per cent
● Liver diseases: hepatitis, jaundice, cirrhosis

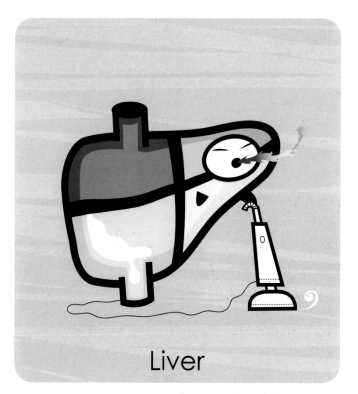

Liver

Kidney
Body Bits

* ☀ Filter that cleans the blood several times a day
* ☀ Along with the bladder, this fellow runs your body's waterworks
* ☀ Takes excess water out of the body

I'm one of a pair of dark red, bean-shaped organs that lurk in your midriff, towards the back. Although I live in a backwater, I provide an essential service. Your body creates a lot of waste every day, most of which ends up in the blood. I filter the blood and offload the waste on Bladder. Sometimes my filters get blocked with chalky stones – ouch!

Kidney

* ● Blood processed per day: 1750 litres
* ● Urine made per day: 1.5 litres
* ● Record no. of kidney stones: 4504

Bladder
Body Bits

☀ Holds your urine in an inflatable bag until it's time to "go"
☀ Urine trickles down to me from the kidneys through two tubes
☀ When full, a valve of muscle opens to release the flow

Bladder

I'm best mates with the kidneys and together "wee" make a good team – geddit? I store the urine, which is yellow because of waste from red blood cells, and it is a good job I'm not obsessed with my size, as I swell up like a balloon. When I'm full, an inner valve opens automatically. Then you'll get that urge. It's up to you to open the outer hatch when ready.

● Bladder capacity: 400 ml
● Urine is 96 per cent water
● It's time to go when bladder is half-full

Skin

Body Bits

☀ A flexible friend keeping you connected to the outside world
☀ A self-mending fabric that responds to changing conditions
☀ Hot stuff that can sweat 2 litres of water every hour

I am the single most advanced material known to humankind – hardwearing, waterproof, super-stretchy and incredibly sensitive. I'll also keep you warm or chill you out and I'm your first line of defence against sticks, stones and infectious diseases. If I get bumped or gashed, I swell up to see off the threat and blood rushes in to form a crusty barrier in the wound.

On my surface, all the cells are dead – you are always carrying about 2 kg of dead skin – but I renew myself every month. If you get cold or frightened, my army of hairs are raised aloft by a team of tiny muscles – they literally give me goose bumps. Below the surface, I'm packed with sensors that pick up pain, cold and heat. My sweat glands cool me down, while oil glands keep me supple.

● Total surface area: 1.9 square metres
● Average weight: 3000 to 4000 g
● No. of bacteria per square cm: over 7.5 million

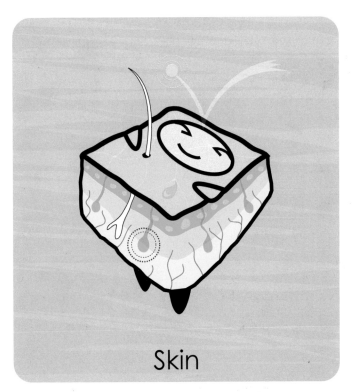

Skin

Nails

■ Body Bits

☀ Hard-bitten guys growing at the end of your fingers and toes
☀ Sharp-suited chaps made from the protein keratin
☀ Despite the rumours, they don't keep growing after you die

Built to scratch, pinch and gouge, we're some of the toughest guys in the body. But due to our brittle personality, we usually crack under pressure. Made from the same stuff as gorgeous Hair, we're her rough little brothers and are as hard as, well, nails. We may be tough, but we like to look our best. Keep us trim and nicely shaped – but remember, don't bite!

Nails

● Growth rate: 3 mm per month
● Longest fingernails: 7.51 m
● Animals with nails: all primates

Hair
Body Bits ■

* Curly, wavy or straight lengths made of keratin
* Grows out of hair follicles embedded in the skin
* Stronger than a copper wire of the same thickness

Hair

I grow mostly on the head to keep it warm – it can get cold up there without me. But you can find me almost everywhere – not just in the shower plughole – but over the rest of your body, except your lips, palms and the soles of your feet. Half of you try to get rid of me wherever I crop up, while the other half unhappily count every strand of me that falls from your heads.

● No. of hairs on head: 90,000 to 150,000
● Growth rate: 1 cm per month
● World record for long hair: 5.627 m (China)

Chapter 4
Green Shoots

This gang of green fiends is intimately involved in the private life of almost everything alive on this planet. Over 90 per cent of the 75 billion tonnes of living things on Earth is greenery. These veggies are the silent heroes of life. They do all the hard work of capturing the Sun's energy and turning it into food. Without them, animals and other living things would have nothing to eat. The green team also flood the air with life-giving oxygen for us to breathe. All plants, such as ferns, fir trees and flowers, are made out of the same type of Plant Cell, but some of this clean-cut crew are found only in Flowering Plants.

PLANT CELL

CHLOROPHYLL

LEAF

STEM

ROOT

FLOWER

POLLEN

SEED

FRUIT

Plant Cell
Green Shoots

* An all-action hero who runs the show inside plants
* All plant parts are made from this mighty, mini building block
* Water is crammed inside to make this guy a really solid chap

I am nothing less than the hub of all plant life on Earth. A versatile all-rounder, my all-purpose body is equipped to build all the parts a plant needs. I may be a tiny tot, but I keep myself in shape – usually a solidly-built box with stiff cell walls. This allows me to stack together in many different shapes and, because I can split myself in two, it's easy for plants to grow new parts.

My secret is that I am crammed with all sorts of useful odds and ends called organelles. These crack troops make plants tick. Chloroplasts, for example, are chock-full of Chlorophyll for converting the Sun's energy; Mitochondria provide the power; the nucleus coordinates the activity. But I'm literally a sap – there's a big sac, or vacuole, in my middle, and it's full of juicy sap!

● Discoverer: Robert Hooke (1665)
● Average size: 10 to 100 x 10^{-6} m
● Types of plant cell include: leaf, stem, root

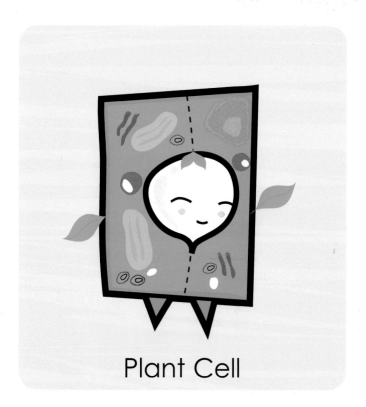

Plant Cell

Chlorophyll
Green Shoots

* The green stuff that makes life on Earth possible
* Found in chloroplasts inside plant cells
* Uses sunlight to make sugary plant-food, by photosynthesis

I'm a miracle molecule who's fantastic at absorbing light. My talent might even make me the single most important chemical on the planet. I drink in energy from the Sun and use it to power the production of sugar – food for a plant and ultimately for all things on Earth, too. As if this wasn't enough, the process (called photosynthesis) also produces the oxygen all animals breathe, and sucks up the nasty greenhouse gas carbon dioxide.

I put the "green" in greenery. I live inside chloroplasts, tiny little green blobs rammed inside the cells of leaves. Because I absorb blue and red light, but not green – which is reflected back – I give plants their colour. In autumn, many plants get rid of me, and their leaves turn a golden yellow.

● Discoverer: Hans Fischer (1940)
● No. of versions of chlorophyll: 6
● No. of chloroplasts that would fit on a full stop: 10,000

Chlorophyll

113

Leaf
Green Shoots

* A Sun-loving lounger that collects the energy used by a plant
* Has been growing on plants for at least 400 million years
* Usually flat and wide to help catch the Sun's rays

It's a tough life being a Leaf. My job is to bask in the Sun all day, soaking up as much light as I can. Ah! Sounds like bliss, but I'm no slouch. I make all the food for a plant.

I'm more organized than you might think. I'm positioned so I don't block out the light for other leaves and I can't be too heavy, so I have a super-light internal skeleton.

I also do the "breathing" for a plant, absorbing carbon dioxide through tiny pores on my surface. I often have a wax coat to stop water loss. Because I'm full of sugar, I make a tasty treat for sheep, insects and humans, so I sometimes defend myself with poisons and stinging spines. You're not the only one who hates hearing the words "Eat your greens!"

● Largest leaves: a type of raffia palm, *Raffia regalis* (24 m long)
● Leaves per tree (oak): 200,000
● Leaf weight (oak): 1.6 tonnes over 60 years

Leaf

Stem
Green Shoots

☀ This upstanding chap uses cellulose to stiffen plant cell walls
☀ Always on hand to make sure nothing droops
☀ A sucker who helps transport a plant's liquid lunch

I'm a stiff sort of fellow, who gets the thirsty work done for plants. I take water to Leaf and his friends and deliver food in the form of syrupy sap. The plant cells I use are harder than most, with woody walls that make excellent tubes for slurping up liquid and making a plant stand to attention. Unfortunately, this stiff stuff also makes vegetables stringy.

Stem

● First plants with stems: ferns
● Longest stem: 112 m (redwood trees)
● Edible stems include: celery, rhubarb

Root

Green Shoots

* The first thing a new plant does is to put down roots
* These hairy suckers get all the best stuff out of the ground
* Evaporation from leaves pulls water up through the plant

Root

Shy, retiring and very down-to-earth, I prefer to bury myself in my work and not show my face. Doing the donkey work, I take up water and essential minerals from the soil, and provide a solid base for future growth. I also store any spare starch and sugar in bulbous underground tubers, such as potatoes, carrots and turnips, which humans love to dig up and eat.

● Root depth record: 68 m (Shepherd's tree, Kalahari desert)
● Edible roots: yams, ginger
● First root to grow from seed: radicle

Flower
Green Shoots

* Flowering plants use this blooming beauty to spread pollen
* Collects pollen from other flowers using a sticky stigma
* If fertilized by pollen, the ovary swells into fruit with seeds inside

Reproductive and seductive, I'm a temptress with one thing on my mind – to spread copies of myself far and wide. I come clothed in the loveliest of colours, with a fiendish array of love traps, perfumes and sweet, sweet nectar to lure insects, birds and even bats to help me complete my mission. Humans use me as a token of love. I'm so beautiful that I'm scientifically proven to make people smile.

As well as my petals, I also have male bits called stamens, which produce pollen, and a female bit called a pistil (made of a stigma and ovary). A pollen cell from another flower tunnels into the pistil to reach an ovule inside my ovary. The two combine to make a seed. Then my pretty parts die, and my leftovers grow into fruit.

* Largest flower: *Rafflesia arnoldii* (1 m)
* *Rafflesia* flower weight: 11 kg
* *Rafflesia* scent: rotting flesh

Flower

Pollen
Green Shoots

* Golden dust that fertilizes a flower's ovule
* Made by the male parts of flowers and causes hay fever
* Eaten by bees and other insects

Tough and intrepid, I'm all man. My mission is to find the female parts of plants of my species and fertilize them to make seeds. But I get up the noses of some people and even make them cry. Let me set the record straight.

One way of getting around, if you are microscopically small like me, is to be blown about in the air. S'not funny for hay fever sufferers! Insects visiting flowers for nectar get me stuck to their legs and I end up on the gooey tip of a pistil. Then my coat cracks open and I drill into the ovary to help make a Seed. My outer coat is so tough that I last for thousands of years. Archaeologists use me to find out what plants prehistoric people used. Because my spiky coat sticks to clothing, I can also be used to place the bad guys at the scene of a crime.

- No. of grains per flower: approx. 7000
- Pollen causing hay fever: grass, oilseed, birch
- Max. distance travelled: 4800 km

Pollen

Seed
Green Shoots

* A tough nut made inside the centre of flowers
* Used by plants to grow new copies of themselves
* Clothed in a resilient jacket and built to last for years

I am the great hope, a parcel that contains everything needed to make a new plant, sent out to colonize the Earth. I'm tough and can survive without food, water or air for hundreds of years. I am scattered in the wind or hitch a ride on animal hairs with velcro-like hooks. Often I get eaten as part of Fruit, and slip through an animal's guts onto the ground.

Seed

● No. of seeds per plant: 10 to 100,000
● Largest seed: coco de mer (20 kg)
● Longest-lived seed: lotus (700 years)

* Sweet, savoury or sour treat made by flowering plants
* Mostly, the flower's ovary forms the fruit, enclosing the seeds
* This ripe fella gets seeds far away from the parents

Fruit

Don't mix me up with vile vegetables – I'm much sweeter. I'm the plump and juicy flesh that surrounds the seeds. That's why tomatoes and cucumbers are fruits. I am often full of sugar and make a delicious snack (healthy, too!). I don't mind getting eaten – in fact, that's the point. Being swallowed makes sure Seed ends up a long way from his parent plant.

* Heaviest fruit (a pumpkin): 450 kg
* Deadliest fruit: castor bean, source of the poison ricin
* Unusual fruits: mangosteen, ugli fruit, durian

Index

Glossary

Alveoli Tiny bags in the lungs where oxygen passes from the air into the blood.

Antibody A chemical tag that is made by cells in the immune system, such as B-cells. Antibodies stick to viruses and bacteria that invade the body. The antibodies mark the invader for destruction by T-cells.

ATP Short for adenosine triphosphate, the chemical used to store energy in cells.

Billion A thousand million or 1,000,000,000.

Carbon dioxide An invisible gas made from carbon and oxygen atoms. Carbon dioxide is a waste product made by living things as they burn their food fuel. Plants also use carbon dioxide gas to make sugars.

Cartilage A tough, flexible tissue, also known as gristle. Sharks' skeletons are cartilage.

Chloroplast An organelle found in most plant cells, where photosynthesis takes place.

Chromosome A structure in the cell nucleus that holds a fragile DNA molecule. Human cells have 46 chromosomes, but that number varies from species to species.

Cilia Tiny structures that stick out of the side of a cell and waft like hairs. Cilia are used to collect food, sense movements and to push a cell along.

Enzyme Some of life's most important molecules, these proteins control the rates of chemical reactions in the body, making them go millions of times faster.

Fertilize When two sex cells, such as a sperm and egg, fuse together to make an embryo that will develop into a new plant or animal.

Gland A group of cells that release a substance, such as a hormone, into or onto the body.

Immune system The body's protection system, which keeps the body free of disease. Its cells clean out any invaders, such as bacteria and viruses.

Kingdom The largest grouping used to categorize different types of organisms. There are five kingdoms: plants, animals, fungi, protists and bacteria.

Lymphatic system A system that removes a greenish liquid which builds up in the muscles. The liquid, called lymph, drains through a network of vessels. Any viruses or bacteria are filtered out at lymph nodes, before the lymph is dripped slowly back into the blood.

Metabolism The name used to describe all of a body's processes.

Molecule The smallest possible unit of a chemical. If a molecule is broken up into smaller sections it will no longer be the same chemical.

Nucleus A bag at the centre of most types of cells where DNA is coiled up on chromosomes.

Organ A structure in the body that performs several roles. The largest organ in the human body is the liver. Others include the lungs, heart and brain.

Organelle A tiny structure inside the cells of plants, animals, fungi and protists that performs a certain job. Mitochondria and chloroplasts are organelles.

Oxygen An invisible gas that is mixed with other gases in the air. Living things take oxygen from the air to burn the fuel in their food in order to power their bodies.

Glossary

Photosynthesis The process used by plants and some bacteria and protists to turn carbon dioxide and water into sugar using the energy in sunlight. Oxygen is released as a waste product.

Protist One of a kingdom of organisms that normally have bodies made from only one cell. Protist cells are larger and more complicated than those of bacteria, and structured more like animal, fungus and plant cells.

Species A group of living things that look the same and can breed with one another. For example, lions form a species, as do apples and button mushrooms.

Stamen The male parts of a flower, where pollen is produced.

Stigma A sticky tip in a flower, where pollen from another flower is collected.

System A group of organs and tissues associated with a particular body function, that interact with one another. For example, the liver, stomach and intestines are some of the organs that work together in the digestive system.

Trillion A million million, a thousand billion or 1,000,000,000,000.

Urine A liquid waste produced by vertebrates as their kidneys clean the blood.

Vacuole A bag of liquid at the centre of a plant cell. The bag is used as a store of water.

Vertebrate An animal that has a backbone, or spine. Fish, amphibians, reptiles, birds and mammals are all vertebrates.

Zygote The first cell of a new living thing, formed by fertilization. The zygote eventually grows into a full body.